T0090692

Lightwork

Poetry for the sensitive type

NICOLE LOUISE HAY

BALBOA.PRESS
A DIVISION OF HAY HOUSE

Balboa Press books may be ordered through booksellers or by contacting:

Balboa Press
A Division of Hay House
1663 Liberty Drive
Bloomington, IN 47403
www.balboapress.com
844-682-1282

Print information available on the last page.

ISBN: 979-8-7652-2554-7 (sc)
ISBN: 979-8-7652-2553-0 (e)

Balboa Press rev. date: 02/22/2022

Contents

The Feminine Wound

The book is "Boundaries" read it,
she rudely said

A familiar alarm bell went off in my head

I had been here all too often,
perhaps every day of my life

I knew a deluge of cortisol would soon warn me
flee or fight

You're triggered, deep breaths,
I said to myself

Red-faced and hands shaking
I tried to focus on anything else

Do something with your body,
let the adrenaline go

So I started doing squats
and quickly went into a vinyasa flow

"Are you *exercising* right here, right now?"
She seemed quite stunned

Her tone was all aghast;
I felt even more shunned

Shame was the word that resounded in my mind

Not for my social absurdity
but for letting this person cross my lines

Why did I always end up here,
time after time?

There must be some lesson that I was not learning
I pondered this question as my glutes started burning
What a relief, she turned, shook
her head and shut the door
I finished out a set of burpees
then sat down on the floor

Was this some kind of Stockholm Syndrome,
was I under a spell?

The primary person violating my
boundaries knew it too well
And she herself was playing my therapist
Pointing out my weakness,
what a sick twist

Be careful, I cautioned,
why give away all your power?

She is but a mirror,
don't let your heart turn sour

I knew that her journey was not the same as mine
I craved a perspective with no victimizers,
no victimized

If not my fate would continue to be sealed
You are your own betrayer,
that's the wound that has not healed

In the dichotomy of winners and
losers that I would create
It was I who always lost and abandoned my own sake
How could I unlearn this way that didn't serve me?
I needed a new definition of power,
one that I could not see

3

Was it culture, the patriarchy,
my own ambition or pride

That had held me captive and limited my mind?
She continued to elude me,
the Feminine Divine

I desired to know her peace,
her harmony

Her mutual uplifting like the waves of the sea
The joy of sisterhood,
the celebration of being a mother

The depth of holding so closely the heart of another
A tear touched my cheek and a
new courage birthed inside
I was no longer willing to abide
This part of me that needed to break free
From the wounded feminine,
the competition, the hierarchy

I opened the door that she had shut,
my hero's journey

And somehow my voice sounded kind,
sincere, with yearning
"That was quite a moment we gave
each other back there"
She stopped typing and swiveled in her chair
Our eyes locked,
defenses started to erode

"I propose that we live by a new code"
"What if you and I start to play on the same team?"
She relaxed her shoulders,
"I know exactly what you mean"

With that one brave gesture of vulnerability
We began a circle,
a flowery opening

And that opened flower grew and grew in might
It seeded others,
gestated by moonlight

A tribe of queens,
artworks of ebb and flow

Shamans of emotions,
big hearts fully exposed

Those queens they danced,
they built, they spoke

They healed with hugs,
those powerful antidotes

Their tears and laughter fertilized the earth
To mystical wonders they gave birth
And from the flowers that began to grow
A garland was woven to crown the earth's glow
A celestial womb that nurtures the world
An orb of enchantment whose story is now being told
In a circle of sisterhood rooted in the earth's core
A circle whose remnants can be
found in ancient folklore
That speaks of a subliminal time and a space
When the Feminine rises,
the Phoenix, fire and grace

Her Shoreline

Her shoreline it has changed
with the ebbing of the tide

Jagged edges now made smooth
High points now sagging lines
And yet with these new soft spaces
A sanctuary has grown
To showcase all her wonders
And provide the birds a home
Her hidden treasures of the deep
Now beckon sun-kissed skin
These waters will rock you to sleep
Come cross the waves, dive in
Explore the sky through his beloved mirror
While light and blissfully you float,
be still and you can hear her

Calling like a siren

That welcomes weary swimmers

Feel the freedom of thought-free mind

Touch the moonlight's shimmer

Plunge into her depths

Hold her and be held

Like a lover, a mother, and a sage

The three in one now meld

New Man

New Man get down off the shelf
We have waited too long for you to show yourself
Appear to us with your sword in one hand
A rose in the other, its soft petals land
At the feet of the feminine, an endless offering
Of tender care and the promise of spring
Let winter's cover cloak the seeds
Of love that you sew, an endless offering

New Man refuse to hurt yourself
Suppressing emotions, your heart let it melt
With vulnerability, embrace the feelings you've felt
No longer a victim of a hand that was dealt
Accept your shadow and your shame
No longer look for her to blame
Follow the grey wolf to the brink of addiction
And earn back her trust with heartfelt conviction

You are strong co-creator, take pride in yourself
No longer a victim of a hand that was dealt

New Man rise like the sun in the sky
Bow down at dusk to the moon, let her rise
Prepare the earth for the abundance you bring
To the feminine's altar, a precious offering
Of harvest you reap, as she destroys and births anew
A cycle you cherish, Gaia's story true
Take your sword to the root of
the trees poisoned by lies
And defend against those who harm in disguise
Surround her home with pink
light, bliss, and empathy
A token of your love for her, a precious offering

New Man rain down wholeness and health
Bring her the sustenance of riches and wealth
Not only material goods but heartfelt connection
Evading the trap of coveted perfection
Find in her your purpose, completion, unity
Give and receive, then again give and receive

Reject the bitter lie of the wound begun by Eve
Instead heal your self-betrayal, take full responsibility
Own who you are and envision who you want to be
Love actualized, this is your offering

Music

I watch you move and it's as if
A song arises from your feet
instead of your lips
When I see you
A melody I see
Of power, hope, and sensitivity
Your feet they glide
As one who walks on the sea
Superhuman, heroic
The waves your symphony
Your body attuned to the ocean
You are poetry in motion
Your arms they sway
Like the willow in the wind
Mothering, nurturing
Welcoming in
The night it resides in the depth of your eyes

Profound and intuitive
The mystic inside
Your hands showcase strength
And at once a grace
As elegant as diamonds and lace
Your fingers they are mesmerizing
Long and noble, hypnotizing
From your lips escapes a note
An ethereal message that an angel wrote
The crown of your head bespeaks that of a queen
Magical, a garland of starlets' sheen
Your song is at once strong and fragile all the same
Vulnerable and open,
yet tuned to ears who have gained
A path to hear the spirit realm
The dimension where you travel
Flowing, glowing with moonlets around
Hidden truths unravel
When I see you it is as if through a thin veil
Of water, of glitter,
of glass sprinkled with shell

I know if I reach out to touch that whispy film
Your skin I will not feel, but dreams
and strength of will

Communicated through vibrations that will not let go
First your soul sung aloud, then mine, its echo
In that duet, I find communion, harmony
As the music lifts upon the air,
I find my sanctuary

But in truth,
I would rather linger at the veil upon my visit

Because to watch you live your aria
is to honor the exquisite

Just One More

It's time to come inside for the night
It is getting cold and we are losing daylight
But I am having so much fun
I can't believe the day is done
Is it really nighttime already?
Can I just play until dinner is ready?
Just one more time down the slide
One more turn for me to hide
Just one more pretend dinner to make
I am cooking dirt, stones and steak
Just enough time for one more of all those
I'll watch from the window to keep you close
Come here, one more hug before you go
One more "I love you so"

It's time to go to bed sweetpee
Clean up all your toys with me

I can help, but you must stop
Your playing, it is way past eight o'clock
Just one more piece of puzzle to place
One more rocket taking off for outer space
Just one more house to construct
One more baby who needs her blanket's tucked
Just enough time for one more of all those
One more time to tickle your toes
Come here, one more hug before the rocket blows
One more "I love you so"

It's time to go to school kiddo
Time to learn, expand, and grow
Would you please clean off your plate?
Grab your backpack we are going to be late
Just one more bite of my breakfast real quick
If I don't eat enough, you know I'll feel sick
Just one more bite or even take a few
Here I'll come sit next to you
Alright you're done, a big hug before we go
And in case you forgot, one more "I love you so"

It's time to grab your bags and hit the road
Time to live in the books and
watch your future unfold

Your roommate should be waiting once we arrive
Oh I miss those college years, I felt so alive
Just one more peek at the room,
it takes me back in time
Oh look, there's the stuffy I was trying to find
Here let me give Pepper's nose one more kiss
I hear the dog is who I will most miss
Just one more minute, actually, take your time
It is hard to leave the past behind
I see those tears, come here, a hug before we go
For the last time to you as a girl,
you know "I love you so"

It's time, they are starting the music soon
The sanctuary is full, there is nearly
no space in the room
Just one more look at you in your dress
My goodness, your man is going to be such a mess
Just one more glance into the mirror
I do love the way that this beading shimmers
One more sip of this champagne
Good thing we chose inside, it is starting to rain
Just enough time for one more of those things
I will check to make sure about the rings
But wait, one more hug before I go

One last time to tell the beautiful
bride, "I love you so"

It's time to push, the baby is ready
Just squeeze my hand and keep
your breathing steady
Just one more contraction before you give in
I know that your head is beginning to spin
Just one more second, let me catch my breath
I want to take advantage of this little rest
Just one more tremor to feel inside
I am biting down and my teeth starting to grind
Just enough time, you can mentally prepare
Oh look, I can see a small patch of hair
She's here! You did it! I'll hug you
both before they make me go
And so you hear it as a new Mommy, "I love you so"

It's time for us to say our goodbyes
I know, there's no way that we won't both cry
The doctor says that I don't have long
Come close here, let's hum our favorite song
Just one more memory for us to make
One more picture in your mind as a last keepsake
Just one last time to hold close my little girl

You know that you have always been my whole world
There's enough time Mom, it's not really a goodbye
I'll think of you underneath every blue sky
Snuggle in here, and tell the angels hello
As I whisper one last time in your ear,
oh how "I love you so"

When You Are Beyond Reach

I love you more than words can say
Love you with these words today
Love you through all time and space
And I love you back again

I love you as the sun does rise
Love you underneath grey skies
Love you even in disguise
And I love you back again

I love you as the moon pulls the tide
Love you though you try to hide
Love you through the pain I will abide
And I love you back again

I love you over, backwards, and under
Love you like the rumble of thunder
Love you as rain clinging to the windowpane
And I love you back again
I love you high up in the trees
Love you in the prayers I plead on my knees
Love you even when you cannot be pleased
And I love you back again

I love you as the storm starts its approach
Love you when the wall is too high to broach
Love you as hysteria starts to encroach
And I love you back again

I love you as your memory fades
Love you with a love that spans all days
Love you even when you don't remember my name
And I love you back again

I love you in that soulful place
Love when a smile lights your face
Love you even when I can't feel your embrace
And I love you back again

Enchanted

My enchantress, how can I resist you?
Though I fight with all my strength,
I am pulled ever towards you

Your charm it has me wrapped around your finger
In your soft embrace I long to linger
But I cannot give in so quickly
When I do, I know that sleep will come swiftly
Tempt me, seduce me, come and kiss me
When I break away, I know you will miss me
I am forever your pursued
A gazelle in the forest, your artist's muse
I want this union, this slumber, this rest
But first I must put you to the test
Is what you offer as sweet as the dream?
Is the peace I imagine as good as it seems?

In truth, I am afraid that it may be so
And in giving in to my death I will go
Come close and whisper your name oh so tender
My name, you answer, is sweet, sweet surrender

The Things I See

The things I see they exist in another dimension
They are beyond the pale,
things no one wants to mention

The things I see they appear as
colors, lights, and figures
Spirits taking animal shape, eagle men, small angels
The things I see they have not happened yet
I know they will
Although perhaps in a different way
Should my vision prevent their ill
The things I see they have personality
Comforting, whimsical, mischievous, pretty, ugly
Little brats and elegant hats
Floating on clouds and flying
When I tune in, I can hear them
As if the Universe is sighing

Not typical sounds as we listen to here
But a message that stems from one's presence
A message I work to make clear
Always bringing with it a lesson
Sometimes one of peace, sometimes one of strife
Sometimes portending the beginning or end of a life
An omen, an explanation, an encouraging word
A story that longs to be told and heard
But never enough my curiosity to satisfy
I am only given one piece of the puzzle,
I remain yet mystified
And in the mystic, that cloudy haze

On these shamanic journeys,
the truth breaks through our chains

It is in this other dimension that all
healing first commences
In this place beyond the pale,
things no one wants to mention

The Swallowed Sun

I swallowed the sun
And disrupted my natal chart
Now instead of a bleeding one
I have a burning heart
I hoped to keep it close
Intimacy my desire
But the sun it now resents me
It feels that I'm a liar
I live with a rage that rises up in my chest
It's the swallowed sun, unexpressed
There is a block in my throat,
scarred tissue from the event

And words on the tip of my tongue that taunt me,
words unspent

Perhaps if I could give it the audience it craves
Not the blue sky overhead,
but a friend to pass the days

Mercury, that closest kin,
she's witty and good with words

I'll swallow her tomorrow
and the two friends will then feel heard
I might stay home just in case
To see what toil swallowing the Messenger makes
But I am determined to make up for what I have done
At least in part,

I am still not willing to free the swallowed sun

Besides, how could I even purge it from my body?
It seems like amputation
Perhaps I'll just say sorry
I can live with heartburn, constipation, restlessness
I think keeping the status quo is probably what is best
Plus, once I give in to the demands
of the swallowed sun
It is a slippery slope,
all my insides could come undone

For example my heart,
it wants feeling and a stage

But no matter, I heard that deep
breathing dissipates the rage
And a lightbulb just went off
I'll freeze my heart to stop the burning
Maybe that will end the torment
of all this pent-up yearning
But can a heart that is frozen still keep me alive?
I'm not asking for amazing, just to survive
What is needed to maintain my vital signs?
The bare minimum is what has kept me thus far safe
It is dangerous, as you know, to
look the sun in its face
But if the choice is between amputation and death
I suppose I'll free the swallowed sun
Just not right now, not yet

Exercise

Today my neck is sore
Not the muscles, but those things that feel like lines

I strained them doing crunches
Those crunches aren't well designed
I was supposed to use my abs
But my head is just connected
More directly to my neck
And so those muscles, or lines, in
my neck were affected

At first, I was disappointed
I wanted a flat mid-drift
But then I saw my recessed chin
Had gotten a little lift
Imagine that, I thought to myself
Was it genius or collateral damage?

My body knew to use my workout
To its greatest advantage
So now I sit here wondering
As I stretch down to touch my toes
Where will I feel sore tomorrow?
In my bottom, back, or...nose?

Stuck

I am a yo-yo

A yo-yo that has gotten stuck

In mid-air I dangle

I cannot move down or up

Whoever wound me must have tangled up my string

I feel taut and tight

Instead of long and lean

I want to stretch from here and

reach down to the floor

I want to spring up again and to the sky then soar

Try as I might, I cannot budge from my position

It seems I have no choice but to change my mission

Rather than a yo-yo with a knot that won't break free

I will be an ornament—

hang me on your Christmas tree

Broken Shell

A little boy walked alone on a beach
A seashell ahead he was trying to reach
He scooped down to pick up the glistening conch
When a heron swept down and the shell did abscond
With the prized possession the boy ventured to find
Found and then lost,
he ran frantically behind

That heron who veered back and forth on the sand
The boy began to despair when he saw start to land
Pieces of that seashell,
his disappointment turned to hope

Pieces that glistened just the same he did note
He ran and picked them all up with great glee
Devoted to take with him some piece of the sea
And just as he gathered all those pieces together

A magical thing occurred,
together they tethered

Within moments that seashell was whole as at first
The heron smirked on a log where he perched
He met eyes with the boy,
eyes full of mischief and secrets
The boy understood at once he was meant to keep it
With wonder and awe he began to grab others
But this time the heron could not be bothered
This one seashell was his one story to tell
A story that only he and the heron knew well
Of manifestation, disappointment and loss
Then faith in rebirthing something
from what was tossed
Aside, because broken the value seemed gone
When really the value maintained all along
And in fact in the healing,
the seashell became one-of-a kind

Priceless, a piece the boy could not leave behind
This seashell he would cherish,
as well as this place

A seashell that he co-created by grace

The Queen

There in the woods in its small, cozy cove
The white rabbit hovered around its warm stove
Hoping that the smell of the meal that it was heating
Would greet wandering companions
looking to come eating

The comfort of rabbit's small stead
Was safe, secure, and boring
Loneliness had set in,
leaving only vicarious living

The forest paths leading out from this humble abode
Were where all creatures big and small
off on adventures rode

An eagle's cry awakened rabbit from its weariness
The wooden spoon fell on the ground,
rabbit looked out for the eagle's nest

Then down one path between the bushes,
rabbit saw a glimmer

Of a gold and silky robe,
the trees around it shimmered

The gold awakened rabbit and for
the first time since arriving
Rabbit saw the crossroads where it had been residing
No longer able to remain,
rabbit timidly pursued the woman

Who wore the robe that shimmered,
who was this regal human?

A game she played with rabbit,

hide and seek of sorts

Rabbit followed deep into the
woods until it reached a fork
A fork in the road that led either further into the thick
Or towards a light,
bright opening with sand and dust and mist

The queenly woman beckoned,
calling rabbit towards the light

Rabbit had never ventured into the open,
the expanse blurred rabbit's sight

But grasping all that shimmered,
that golden cape that glowed

Was too magnetic to reject,
so onward rabbit followed

The sand it tickled rabbit's feet,
the white light warmed full body

The daring nature of its quest made
rabbit feel quite naughty
Suddenly the mist gave way to a magical hot springs
Aqua water oh so clear,
nature's spa refreshing

The golden lady beckoned rabbit
as she waded into the water
Timid rabbit tested a toe,
wishing it was hotter

A surge of panic and thrill surged through
A decisive moment, rabbit knew
Hesitation froze rabbit still
No going back, nor forward until
Her fingers outstretched grazed rabbit's coat
Electric as if rabbit received a jolt
Of courage, valor, sheer impetus
Into the water rabbit then burst
Cold at first, then comforted
Rabbit floated, splashed, and spinned
Onto its back, gazing up at the clouds
Then rolling, plunging round and round
That electric shock then struck again
This time through rabbit's ears
The golden lady now face to face
Kept pulling and pulling rabbit nearer
Deeper, deeper down they went
Rabbit was frightened and disoriented
Until a luminescence appeared,
an underwater current

That current whisked them through
an underground cave
Of monuments and arches
In a moment of reprieve, a blessed breath it gave

A cavern of fresh air and marshness
That current then thrust rabbit down again
This time rabbit gave in with glee
Through another underwater
passageway rabbit went
Rainbow light was all to see
Rabbit rode through the rainbow
The light so penetrating
Out popped rabbit into white waters rushing
Towards a waterfall, no escaping
Rabbit lifted arms preparing for the fall
Lifting its chin up towards the sky, it gave a joyful call
Those arms no longer furry white
Now human, golden, ladylike
Transformed into the shimmering Queen
By the rainbow light
She hit the waterfall's end
Plunging into the depths
Of another wading pool
This one pure transcendence
Long and elegant she emerged
Now glistening herself
And towards the ocean she then turned
Full radiance she felt

Her bronzed feet sparkled in the sand
Her robe a sashaying whisper
Red nails adorned her gorgeous hands
Her hips they all but lifted her
Lightly off the ground
Up to reach the sun
Warmed in places lost and found
Her hair unkempt, undone
There at the shore's edge the Queen she rested
Lying atop a sandy bed
A dark Adonis she manifested
He strode up and lifted her head
Just enough to savor her
To introduce himself
He exuded all her pleasure
A man full of emotional wealth
With seductive fervor
Their rainbow lights did blend
Connecting all the crevices
Open hearts and hidden dens
At last the goddess fell asleep
Drifting on a cloud to slumber
Left to dream of a white rabbit
And a past life full of wonder

Printed in the United States
by Baker & Taylor Publisher Services